D0555145

BITE DOWN LITTLE WHISPER

BITE DOWN LITTLE WHISPER

Don Domanski

BRICK BOOKS

Library and Archives Canada Cataloguing in Publication

Domanski, Don, 1950-, author
    Bite down little whisper / Don Domanski.

Poems.
ISBN 978-1-926829-86-9 (pbk.)

    I. Title.

PS8557.O43B58 2013   C811'.54   C2013-903712-8

Second Printing - October 2013

We acknowledge the Canada Council for the Arts, the Government
of Canada through the Canada Book Fund, and the Ontario Arts
Council for their support of our publishing program.

The author photo was taken by John Proctor.

This book is set in Minion Pro, designed by Robert Slimbach and
released in 1990 by Adobe Systems.

The cover image is by Don Domanski.

Design and layout by Cheryl Dipede.
Printed and bound by Sunville Printco Inc.

Brick Books
431 Boler Road, Box 20081
London, Ontario N6K 4G6
www.brickbooks.ca

Contents

THE LIGHT OF UNOCCUPIED MEMORY

For Mary

... there is only one subject ... this indivisible subject is every being in the universe and these beings are the organs and masks of divinity.

~ Jorge Luis Borges

FORESIGHT BY EARTH

URSA IMMACULATE

night swept back over the headlands
someone's sign language alone in the forest
scratching words in the air   haunting
narrow spaces between the pines

hieroglyphical pheromones carried on the breeze
anagrammatical gestures almost apparitional
                                almost perceptible

midnight and a redtail asleep in his negative theology
luciferin shine of fireflies   a coyote folding the pleats
of her wound   swaying her god with the pain
with the suffering that falls through belief's chasm
that small caesura between flesh and bone

I've been sitting alone beside the lake   subbing
for a rock or a blade of grass   watching
the phrase *ex nihilo* feather the water's surface
and faces of the Julii shine out from drab houses
                                of the midge larvae

the moon puts on a clean white shirt and rises
I lean back into the blood of my shoulders
and neck   into the pure vowels of my spine
vocalic pins attaching vertebrae to nerves
what was mutely sung by everything nameless
                                everything forgotten.

*

solitude is our nourishment and redemption
in a world that is sensed rather than understood
quietude our reprieve from the skin-trade
of language   so I come to seek refuge here
in the stillness spreading among evergreens
like the dissemination of algae   like nightjars flying
through first kisses and Chinese whispers

we should confine ourselves to the present
as Marcus Aurelius wrote   but it's a hard sell
when memories like pollen set ablaze
                         fall from the air
with their final wish for us in hand
reddening the meditative colours
of each moment   white and off-white
pearly counterpoint to words and meaning
moony phosphorescence in the marrow

moonlight makes the world seem more absent
the blood of things more secretive and present
phenomena hushed and all breathing space
lit by a saurian light   bioluminescent glow
in the brain stem   our reptilian brain
like a pre-existent prayer that sometimes
rises out of story and flesh

I stand up and walk along the water's edge
beside me a heron's footprints run line after line
like typographical errors in the glistening mud
above me moths chaperone the musculature
of stars and the Delphic shudder of a cloud
           prophesying a bright green world

it's difficult to know the sanctitude
of things   bloodsqualls metabolized
hatched and cross-hatched   blackened down
                        to flesh and gesture
hard to imagine all the tongues tied in the weeds
all the heartbeats time-lapsed beneath each stone
life incessantly singing to itself in the night
funereal lips and luminous throats

it's difficult to know the sanctitude
of ourselves   as we breathe the rapture of time's
cadences deep into our lungs   along with the given
sum and cipher of human concerns
downshifting them through vein and bone
our entire lives magnetized to a shining point
each day   able to be carried away with a sigh

in the end being human is a long and wordless
journey   ask the dead caught and released
along the margins of a stag's breath
ask them as they descend the wooden steps
of the birch trees   that go far underground
till they reach Ursa Major   Ursa Immaculate
                        Bear of the Clear Heart.

                        *

walking along the shore   every footstep
a homecoming   every blade of bracken
                        with a finger to its lips
the earth imagining a physical world
my body shoulder-deep in a Dantean fluidity
In the middle of my life, I went astray
and I awoke in a dark wood

in the middle of my life I'm standing
next to the quillwort   listening
to nettles grind their teeth   to saplings
asleep in their future branches
to my every thought like a breath
loosened from a windowpane

this is the hour when Ursa Major comes as
a supplication   stars like bees sworn to light
when all our religions feed the shadows
of uncertainty to its most silent angels
when all our philosophies sound like small
animals beating their children in the grass

this hour is called wearing dark clothes
beneath your skin   this is called walking
through the forest with zero gravity behind
your eyes   this is called sign language
without an owner   emptiness of this hour
this is called the pale jawline of infinity
and flesh   called opening your mouth
without a sound.

GLORIA MUNDI

To the sleeper, alone, the animals came and shone
~ Josephine Jacobsen

early November   no narratives left
in the dead grass   backyards
beginning to hold our afterlives
a little frost haunting its own white hair
the dead envious   watching the endless
youth of dust settle on everything

bare trees weighted down with crows
and another planet's moonlight
a mouse's shiver in the fallen leaves
its pins and needles out of whack

shadows of the Pleiades under seven stones
feral cats moving about on paper cuts
no bats to sieve the air   no oracles
to predict what tenderness will do

the bodies of crickets lay ungathered
their prayers were like ours   cislunar
held in place by fear and doubt
never arriving at any destination

night came smoothly with a low growl
like the muscles of a bestiary pulling
its covers shut and the glory of the world
became disembodied   weightless
above your pure wish to be secure

bedtime and now the animals will arrive
claws and fur and geomorphic skins
all beside you   all warming you
with their bodies of switchback flesh
                        and rheumy bones

close your eyes   unclench your hands
dreams come through the maternal line
and clouds are our mother tongue
go to sleep   repeat after them.

sunlight bright on pine boughs   saints asleep in the Great Bear
the Great Bear asleep in North Mountain   everything waiting
for the next words to be spoken   something to stir water and gravel
to braid soil and light   a few phrases left over
from the creation of the world and its sparrow's heart.

*

Tuesday   blank hours of summer lazing in the heat
time presupposes time   endlessness of afternoons lost
in their own alchemical sense of surfaces and shadows
bees hyperkinetic across meadows   each takes at least
sixteen days to make   sixteen afternoons of heaven's push
and heed   transubstantiation   afternoons into flesh
                              flesh into honey.

*

a new day in the Annapolis Valley   crows like prayer wheels
spinning above spruce spires   water bears rehydrated
antsqualls in flight   the calligraphy of a spider's web torn
by the wind   topography of a feather   abandoned shoe
in the mud   its laces tied around the hour   ready to begin
again   to accompany us on our journeys   our little junkets
along the edges of oblivion   treasures of the begotten
and half-begotten   such resplendence   such intransitive
moments   such fortunes near at hand.

*

deadfall of light and its amenities   retinal light leaking into
the blindness of chickweed   white clover leaning
into the sun's maculae   ferns lifting their fronds   rhizomes
sending up parts of speech to answer the call to ascension
chlorophyll our eternal contemporary   old friend with green
raiments and pockets full of maps to places we'll never go
or even think of going   not faraway destinations   just there
in that spot   three feet away.

*

water's shorthand in the gully   its signature carried downstream
countersigned by the river   authenticated by the sea   wave sway
and memory   pointing to the horizon's keel   upturned
and freeze-framed   where the stars abound just beyond the blue
abound and take us in   when no one else will   we live
in meridian light forever   we live our life on a waterdrop
with its young-bearing rapture and weight
Queen of Breath   Madonna of the Diaphanous Life.

*

cliff swallow above the valley floor   her mind a bit of night sky
flying through daylight   galaxies and stars turning   in synch
with her every move   a celestial static around her body and wings
like a steady rain falling inside a cathedral   while on the ground
a bit of moss on a branch   a few green hyphens from a lost sentence
about Heaven's roots in the scenery   about a cloud of mosquitoes
coming back from the other side   with angels on their breath.

*

a vole's divinity beneath the ground cover   blush of isness
in every leaf   the ungod of things holding on to secrets
ministering to the dark and arabesque waters of the past
hue of the curlew's cry   colour of inclement silver   midday
patdown of absence   our absence   our postbeliefs carried
off by the breeze   no one to stand in for us   to take our burdens
down to the river and ferry them along   to take our words away
only the redtail to watch over us   only that redtail and that cloud.

*

a cloud   marl-coloured   a cool rinse drifting along
the whole world listening to its silent approach and fade
little voice   like a pale acolyte from Thrace   lost in prayer
while we align ourselves with a grace that glosses up the sheen
of our disaffections   sitting with weeds and stones
like Skellig monks contemplating the sea   waiting for the future
coming through dry grass   through the split ends.

*

our future waits well beyond our hubris and intent   its pulse
far off and oversewn with foliage   its incremental heartbeat
rising from the forest floor   twice removed from human ken
then twice again   the dead nibble at those roots to no avail
desire pillows its light but finds no resting place   no physic
or balm for our ten thousand vulnerabilities   only the nightly
asceticism of a stargaze into the firmament   into photospheres
and waterdrops   a swallow's mind above the given world.

*

we spend our days wherever we find ourselves   always suited up
in our storylines   with very little to show outside
of language   not even enough to place on our eyelids as we sleep
our sinews and bones jotting down notes   our demise
written in our little catechism of anecdotes   in those sad chapters
dim and vacant as prescriptions from an afterlife   circumstances
wearing us down and away from the earth on every page.

*

there's something about us that inhibits our ability to amend
the stillness to a deeper stillness   to inhabit quietude   to live in
the world   there are not enough reliquaries to hold our saintless
bones   not enough reasons to bring us back from perdition
meanwhile we long and belie that longing   as we write our
confessions   black ink on black paper   meanwhile the sun moves
through nostalgia's ether   meanwhile something has sicced
the dog rose on the bracken and called the chlorella home.

WILDERNESS OF THE RAINDROP

clambering up the bluff   Hokusai's wave behind me now
still moving around the circumference of the earth
still carrying sea glass and dead sailors ashore

the forest comes to meet me at the edge with open arms
and the psalm of a breeze   zephyr of feral sighs
bending being just a bit closer to the ground
closer to the centre of things   to the last light of day

I stand watching the Atlantic darken   watching
the great wilderness of the raindrop   at my feet
a rabbit's skullcap and mouse tibia in the grass
cup white   empty cup and spoon
place setting for one   for the voice that has drifted
far from its body   utterance lost in the undergrowth

up here the lisp of the forgotten can be heard every night
every night the unclottable arteries of the afterlife empty
their black stories onto the rocks below   to be carried
out to sea   to be finned   gilled   deepened by whitecaps
and fathoms   caught in nets a universe away.

Ars Magica

for Miki

amphitheatre of late afternoon   Gallo-Roman wasp nest
humming quietly in the hedge   ghosts stitching water
                                              to the shoreline

these hours like the rough side of a towel against your cheek
pine needles underfoot   already making a path to winter
seated in your garden   lungs hilling breath after breath
eyes following an old crow through the trees
its feathers like worn photographs of flight

you sit with the infinite shadows of four o'clock
with the planetary weight of grass all around you
with machinations of xylems drawing life from stones
clouds coming in from the Atlantic
immaculate longhand of what's never to be written

Quietude is called returning to life Lao Tze says
even on a Tuesday afternoon in Nova Scotia
even with the hood ornaments of chocolate irises
gleaming outward from their arterial darkness
with the unborn standing high up in the trees
                                  like cemetery angels
one finger pointing to heaven   the other to earth

you sit in silence   nothing visible nothing invisible
repose is the art of magic   the subtle gesture offstage
like a pigeon's hymn rising into another life
or spiders squeezing hearts through silk
or gold artifacts under glass
              draining the human world of light.

Bardo

first light of day inscribed on night's gravity
sweet breath of noumena between the pines
this is the path of the unconverted
                    the unwashed
its pentimento showing through
the blood   showing through grass and weeds
                              briar and brush

I made camp just beyond the pond
where algae live happily in the continuous
loop of their wedding nights
just south of where ravens are already flensing
bodies of the departed   and crickets live
with their glassine eyes   their lidless black paper
                              watching the world

all the night shinings go out like candles
two by two   certain eyes close while
others open   as a breeze braids through
the old growth of this hour   sun rising
ur-light giving the sense that everything
is in holy orders   that we all live
in the guise of ourselves   in a measure
          of space under a monk's cowl

pampered bacteria in the leaf mould
dead foxes in their vestments
the grasses' heart stretching on for miles
swamp water living the life of tea steeped
                              to intelligence

the cursive pulse of everything in synch
like a geothermal cipher   warm as a deer's core
and every footstep we take is just where
the world's edge dips into infinite space

this morning I walk carefully there   knowing
that the husks of dead flies and twigs dust
all the rooms of Paradise   that every windfall
apple has come to change the world.

FORESIGHT BY EARTH

1.

a bit of July   a bit of August   a day
                  spent moving about in the overlap

a sky like an amalgam of mercury and tin applied to the backs
of mirrors   everything on earth reflected back to itself
everyone anonymous at least once a day

the 21st century growing like bright apples on dark branches
coddled with meaning   polished and red   cardio red
each carrying cyanide in their seeds   little pills for the voyage.

2.

the day rotates just beyond sight   like Nibiru the invisible planet
like gnosis turning at a cellular level   the day offering itself up
to stillness   to that great lingua franca   connecting all beings
                                        one to the other

like that dragonfly over there orchestrating a red move in blue air
with wings like four photographs of Venice taken from space
it follows emergence   the engendering of silence   genesis of
certitude in every flex of its body

death connects us too   death and silence are harbingers
of a singularity   presage of this moment   the unending epilogue
                                        unceasing mantra
beneath all our mythologies and conjurings death is witching blood
drops yet to fall   silence ready to collect them   absorb them
into the talismanic naught between heartbeats

an ancestor of mine was beheaded in Lyon   killed for her beliefs
by the Inquisition   I have no belief I would die for   none that requires
my demise   I only believe that the Book of the Dead exists somewhere
its pages turned by the scattering and gathering of clouds   by rain drifting
                                        from name to name.

3.

deer are about   practicing geomancy   abiding in *foresight by earth*
walking their ley lines beside the river   their dreamscape   its sighting
lifted up into their bodies with every step   horsetails trampled
algae's piecework spoiled for a moment   light slicked back in the water
                              undercarriages of beetles floating by

whitetails walk about studying the graphology of what's never written
what's almost scripted below the hardpan   the almost of an eating world

in the Upanishads it says *I am food, I am food, I am food! I am the*
eater of food, I am the eater of food, I am the eater of food!
I like the simplicity of that   the beauty   like a Japanese screen carefully
folded shut and laid on the grass   its purpose summed up and done.

4.

the air is untranslatable   Dante's orphanage   *Paradiso*   *Paradiso*
waiting for its theology   its angelology   for the visitation of pure light

we live in the world of the long cloth   of the blindfold wrapped loosely
around landscape and sinew   no surprise that days and nights remain out
of reach   drained by our mission creep towards extinction   by our
ignorance of givenness   no wonder we walk about each day partially erased
that we're unfaithful to the cosmogenic laze of protoplasm   to the vaulting
of baleen   little bell of grass   queue of bloodroot holding the wingbeats
                                            of carinates till they're born.

5.

anthills sitting like Bodhisattvas in meditative postures   tending their
sutras that transcend individuality   meta-fadeaway to absolutes
exoskeletal and dharma-washed   their cognitive content otherwise and pitiless
with only the windfall of death shining forth to enlightenment   their desire
a redshift in the frequency of the air   a low and non-negotiable layering
of votive fires   unlit and uncomforting   no substitute for darkness
                              for the warmth of the unkindled

ants apply their cloistral optics to the landscape   their eyes of irreversible
blackness   their tube-like hearts in their backs   their savage gravitas
ferocious as angels on a pin   little fasteners of the inexplicable
with mouthparts like surgical clamps   holding onto time's flesh
like we do   and like them we never let go   always hoping there's more
to come from what's prescribed   a little respiration to be drawn
from the margins of the air   its remission   its feather and drift.

6.

I stand with an addiction to gravity   supporting my crushed spinal column
my totemic leg gathering pain and pathologies into one clan   a campfire there
someone dancing wildly   sunlight poured out like Medici gold
across the landscape   the sun dominating my sensibilities
all afternoon its sizzle and aura   yet I am also that flame and its implications
each of us a balefire on a distant hill   signalling back to its resolve

grief too shines forth like a great heat   a sublime burn on our skin
which no salve will heal   like incense it fills the sky   so that all the world's
wrongs actualize as dust on tips of grass eventually   immeasurable sorrows
bending in the breeze   swaying in and out of reality   there's no antigen for this
no hex or spell to relieve our bereavements   our injuries like ionized air sheeting
off an electromagnetic field   invisible   continuous.

7.

filigree of bloodlines   a giant net thrown over the earth and its kingdoms
no escape from its euphoria and censure   like monks we come down from
the mountains and return to them   filled with questions   we have our prayers
of course   we have our embellishments   we have the undercoat of texts
to guide us along   words like snagged branches across endless pages
by number and measure the fold-outs open   the maps appear   feather-edged
rough to the touch   X marking the spot where the sparrow fell   where
the birch grew   where we were born   where the darkness first caught up
with us   every X glints on after the covers are closed   after the books
have been shelved   tucked quietly again into darkness.

8.

ravens pick up the conversation and then put it down   their flight jackets
open to the wind   a coyote the colour of Pythia's vapour
glides between spruce trees   his mind wordless and time-neutral
his legs scissoring and unscissoring down to the meadow   where I saw a pair
of rabbits earlier   concealing their contentment   slipping stitches of clover
who knows if they'll survive the day   if they'll see the moon ascend
over the pre-lapsarian sleep of the forest   its infusion and glean

who knows what happens just beyond our lip-synch of breath and blood
what shadows appear just behind our backs   what blank wounds follow
us all of our lives   waiting for their moments of flesh

who knows what celestial numbers enfold us   what sequencing carries us
along   as quietly as the soil's darkened rib cage rising and falling
in the Olduvai Gorge   as gently as the illusory nature of phenomena
our lives almost absent   lived in a brief stay of light

like a dark grace fading into the opulence of landscape

like melancholia accumulating as fine dust on someone else's shadow.

Green Bird

this forest has the weight of a book at rest   one never written
never read   no plot or storyline   no author or cover   only two
fly-leaves and a spine   little green bird you fly away and return
fly away and return   they burn you   they cut you down
                                              and you return.

APOCRYPHA

it begins as stars outsource to morning
and last night's credits start to roll
wrapping up another incomprehensible
cosmology   lights and acknowledgments
                    in dark suspension

it begins as you wake   falling through
the infinite coincidence of the moment
that moment filling with light
and sleep like old teeth in the bark
still gnawing something sweet on the other side

it begins with arthritic water in the drains
and pipes undarkening in expectation of you
when your slippers are the edges
                of all visible things

you start your day   that's when it begins
murmur of voices far off in the wind
votive whispers and their Apocrypha
pure as a dog's bark   as dog hair
brushed off a stone   to drift away.

Magnum Mysterium

I was the one who first placed a pair of eyes
in the darkness   I left them on a large black tree
on a rock face I left an ochre kiss
on each life the awful hush of carbon
on every sensation a perpetual sigh

at the pulse of every red movement in the body
I placed endless blue space to remind it
of death   I placed lungs in fish
and then changed my mind   I sang camarillas
and patted each organ into position around the sun

I was charismatic and circumboreal
a skitter of thoughts   a jangle of namesakes
I was a deep and dark intaglio at the end
of every nerve   a bailiwick at the far end
of every consciousness

I was wilderness   I made orphans out of ascension
I disposed of every elision except absence
and introduced piquerism to insects   flight to stones
I coddled magma and micro-organisms
I added digestion to every biome   a womb to every tooth

I placed God in the details and then said goodbye
I rode the thermals till I was solid   I walked the earth
till I was air   I surrendered only to dirt beneath my nails
to the hard pinch of sight in my head   to my own mystery
the hulking of my tongue   to dung in my hair

I subdued joy in the higher orders and let it grow
wild in the lower   I ran blood through
the stems of butterweed   fire through
the scapulae of rivers   I told the first nouns there
were no verbs   the language believed me
and the language fell down.

Apparitional Hound

for Uisge Beatha

saw you running late last night
a quickening of silver in your legs
gold canticles hanging from around
your neck   every third footstep reaching
the ground   as you travelled to that
unknown place a millimetre away

it's a long journey to the afterlife
where each stone is hand-blown
and lit from within
where the traffic of stillness is deafening
atmospherics shot through with embraces
and requiems

death is just one more lost language
infused with dust   immixed with birdwing
outstretched to a wondrous sheen
just beyond knowing   beyond unctions
and bishoprics

there's a mythos there too   made from
the eminence of animals   a passional of faunae
an ideology of shadows washed into memory
wolves recalling the edges of Sumerian towns
stags remembering the ancient forest
of Khandava   and hounds like you
calling back the wild runs with Herne
on all the back roads of the world

out of time you will knock claws again
into another earth   see stars as whispers
of a deeper illumination   become part
of that bestiary   a newborn tooth
               among infinite teeth
each named by fire   by any measure of light
each drawing blood from paradise.

Night Scroll

nightdrift above the bay
                          land tilting starboard
ocean listing to port
        hundred million brushstrokes of grass
two herons flying past the moon

four steps into the sky   then you're on your own.

The Garden Is Secretive and its Wounds
Are Light to the Touch

for Mary

it's the paper anniversary of the azaleas and you've tended
to their needs   fed their dark hearts   watered their shadows
with your own   while roses stood nearby on cleft feet
their cerebrations collecting as red mist beneath your eyelids

this morning you also transplanted poppies   like moving omens
from one life to another   across the flower bed's immaculata
that elusive presence gardeners feel as they work
                    something just beyond their field of sight
like the predynastic light of Abydos shining out from bare
                         and abandoned places at dusk.

                    *

bright world   Krishna-blue sky   offertory of water and leaves
the air sweet   standing between worlds   between this one
and the next   the gloam waiting offstage   always half awake
half asleep   clouds fastened to a life yet to appear
and you seated there   beneath the red Japanese maple
the border of railway ties behind you   still feeling the weight
of trains   boxcars full of black soil heading for promised land

beside you the narcissi are watching   staring hard into the sun
looking for their second lives and their third   slow blink
slower destinations arriving out of thin air   to carry them away
like us they look to the sky for answers   like them we find none
having only the garden to sustain us   nurture and dilate
our existence for a time   our marginality concealed from us
for a moment or two   our heads bowed   arms at our sides.

                    *

July is immortal   dog days and flower heads   grackles perched
on the ginkgo tree   each an unknown entity wishing to be known
by something beyond its own actions and thought   as we all do
an otherness to embrace us   give us names and send us on to a new
life   the next sultry day just over that green horizon

for you that embrace is blue and engendering   delphinium blue
the feathery blue of jays ciphering from pillar to post
blue wounds of the garden   light to the touch   deeper to the spirit
your blue destiny abiding in the yard's infinity   gathering you in
holding you close   its mossy cheek pressed against yours
one kiss from the earth is all it takes   the only blessing needed
the only potion required   a slight breath   a drop of dew
from tomorrow's sunrise   a drop of blood from yesterday's pain.

*

the garden can't offer us mercy or love   only transcendence
only the renderings of salvation   resurrection and deliverance
it can't protect us   but nothing can   all our charms and amulets
only Braille our flesh   writing things there we'll never understand
with our eyes opened or closed   a few unseeable gestures
is all the universe has for us   the ocean in the stem   meadow
in the blossom   a day of sunlight and a night of sleep

yesterday you stood in the garden as the moon materialized
like Siddhārtha's palace above the mulberry   everything
around you secretive and ghost-edged   hoarding silhouettes
and outlines of a forest beneath your feet   ten hundred feet down
and rising   already ravens and swallows settled in its branches
already wolves and hares move between its trees
the great forest that comes after us
                                wintering in black snow   waiting its turn.

Steel City

for Joseph Sherman (1945–2006)

once in a while I remember the place   sulphur and coal
dust always moving towards form but never arriving
company houses   dark itch of window and door
the High Renaissance colours of tailing ponds

we both grew up there   you went to synagogue   while I
leaned on Jesus for awhile   poetry waiting for us down the line
an art form that began as dog vespers in the empty streets
as blood in the vein   memento mori in the mind   heliocentric
orbits of thought coming to rest each night
                              among fleabane and cracks in the pavement

back then poetry was our footsteps in the rounds of the day
those little falls through the pulse   the candlepower of each one
                              circa then   circa memory
every footfall like a dropped heartbeat   between heartbeats
the drifting clouds   between clouds the flickering self.

IN THE DOORYARD

current of air stirring the hostas   cat asleep beneath
the warmth of a star   bees flying about with bouquets
and hypodermics   lazy hours spread out on the grass
like a thin green blanket   discoloured with minor
activities   with my thoughts and their moving pictures

this would be a good day for dogs to finally stand on their
hind legs and speak   for Fate to answer our questions
for the rapture of childhood to occur again   for God to
lift the veil and show us the inner workings of a stone

like I said lazy hours   nothing much happening   so I do
what I always do   watch things get on with their lives

a young sparrow circling the plastic red birdfeeder
toad on the uncut lawn   carrying its underlife and ashes

a millipede performing its custodial duties in the mulch
its legs in Times Roman   typing its message
into the earth as it walks along   always the same one
for over 400 million years   *keep your feet on the ground*
                                keep your feet on the ground.

FOR THE PURE MOTHER BEE

a breeze like Yahweh's nitrogen-bearing sigh
bending amendments of grass beside the highway
sun sugaring diatoms along the shore
gravitational corridors far off between the trees
carrying dead whitetails away

noon on the backs of bees sweetened by their own dogma
the dampness fading as quietly as the dieback of villages
along the coastline   while we live a life in drowsy
photosynthesis   each day staring into offerings of light
our nights spent mapping those transmutations
multiplying our options till we reach zero

each night we lie in bed with dark graces tattooed
between our vertebrae   black weave
of a black needle in infinite space
we sleep to cross things out   to forget
all our false gods tending their fallen altars
housekeeping beneath hawkweed and woodlice.

*

the hive's horoscope is swollen with honey and wax
Gemini, don't let this year's abundance of possibilities
be tomorrow's lost dreams
but no predictions for this new century or the next
or for the fire ants   little bodice-rippers all in a row

also none for the soothsayers swaddled in elementary forms
over there beside the river   mooning about   rearranging
the birthmarks of stars on ether   holding us up to the light
till we darken and disappear like old paper   old cantos
divided by the slow mime of our lost phrases resurfacing
                                        in someone else's flesh.

we never seem to look closely enough at things
like the waters of the world meeting in every
blade of grass   in every stone a deeper stone
or a bedroom from the 1700s   long gone
drifting above the spruce trees   someone dreaming
there still   counting her one blessing over and over
a breath held   a promise kept

we watch the bees but never really see them
never see that they're old latrias ceaselessly flying
into the wind   that they're the last curve on the road
to the royal line   to the Minoan Pure Mother Bee
that they have the composure of absolution
and its single unending caress   no fear   no regret
their black and gold bodies only stained
                              by tearless things.

*

where the *thou* can take you can't take the bee
the lineage of the *I* dies hexagonally in every cell
we on the other hand practice a self-aesthetic
the words *meadow* and *honey* are just part
of the process of naming our long despair

. we all live beside a dark river   bodies
soaked in the backwash of our cognitive functions
canonized to a point behind our eyes
the saintly pull into nothingness   seraphic iridescence
of empty space between each belief   each decision

we sit staring into the intangible wholeness of light
our thoughts strung along a silk thread
each one a pause in amber   each rubbed to a bruise
our hopes and our fears   the little beads.

A FERAL TRANCE

A Bright Fable in a Dark Wood

what we were meant to see we've seen ten thousand times
sunlight falling on its sword in a hayfield   a craze
                            of birdmaking in the trees
taxonomy of the sadhus drifting by cloud-like and deathless
white pebbles and dandelion globes   little fetishes
and their interwork   carrying our lives on their
small shoulders   those lives we build beyond the event
horizon   so no light or sound escapes from our desires

those contemplative days wrapped around our bodies
                        stellar hours leaning upon us
from out of the blue   from out of the Great Dissolve

what we have longed for we've longed for ten thousand times
no words for this weight upon our hearts
no name for this hospice which has taken us in
                        its gallery of illuminations opened wide
to our gaze   its rooms filled with inklings and quantum fields
our lodgings occupied and shining forth
out of a meadow's breath   where we live in the ecstasy
of asterisms   in the accidental bliss of space-time
woolgathering flesh to bone   holding tight
to elementary particles   to remnants of thought scattered over
the circumference of a blood drop   over the mete of a vein.

                    *

whatever we've done will never be finished   whatever is named
                        is unnamed as soon as we turn away

beneath the sky's sketchbook
we make our plans   we imagine the future under the flyover of stars
lifting their names from a page   chandeliered high above our bodies

we are nothing more than brushwork and pillow talk
living beside the stone's perpetual ascension   beside the moonlight
                              sipping water from the roots of things
lying down our heads to dream of stones and moonlight   every day
collecting dust on our sleeves   every night shaking dirt off our shoes.

                              *

we'd like to be a new parable   we'd like to be a bright fable in a dark
wood   to deepen the range and pulse of our lives   like shadows do
by merely tissuing radiance   colour-coordinated all the way
                              down to the river

unlike the revealed we burrow into our hiding places   unlike
the hidden we draw attention to ourselves   trying to find a niche
in the diminishing circles of our beliefs   following an apparition's
                              prosthetic light just above the trees

we are beautiful and lost   our unknowing raising its hands in prayer
the scriptures of our bodies slowly peeling away in whispers   our words
like the secretive cries of grass torn over and over by the wind
always returning to our sorrow
                              always about to address it but only miming
those hieroglyphics   that melancholic scrawl half erased
                              those eroded depictions of our grief.

dawn   the entire sky softly lit   like Vermeer-light
in the pink braids of a bream's gill
5:45 a.m.   already the disappearance of happy endings
atavistic   buzzed cut   orphaned among quillwort
                                        and Jesus bugs

for hours I've been thinking that the physics of darkness
is a nondescript and unworkable substance   best left
in the blood   along with that thin space between butterfly
and pin   between skin and star   where we build
                            our little houses
pressing them up against the unceasing wind

but daylight is no better   almost blinding
never showing us anything but ourselves
behind the veil   left with only our desires acting like
mnemonic devices   the cosmetics of memory
rubbed into our skin   some rouge   some powder
anything to keep the self full   to stop the mad
mothers in the trees from carrying us away

first crow of the morning high up on a dying spruce
jawing back its words from the day before   taking
back what it said to that eerie sense of itself
a litany of heart-rending points
just beyond its syllabus and voice

a second century night beneath each fallen log
someone always sitting there stirring a fire
our ancestral mothers bent to abacination
their bodies like skeleton keys rusting in the weeds
the door of their breastbones opened long ago
                                        and gone

I want to believe what those women believed
to be open to visitational moments from deep
in the forest   to the quietude lost in the fro
of things   in the whispers of neural firings
that constantly bruise the absence of meaning

I want to be like water with a finger to its lips
saturated with episodes of a soul's shudder
like the lake's mojo finding its resting place in
its own deep spell   I want to disremember
just below the surface of water's arrhythmia

I want to be open to everything that is wayward
and lost   even to the axons' apparitions
crisping back to another form of flesh
to an almost mortal life   almost lived again

I want to disremember as I walk through this field
through this first folio of the unwritten
each of my footprints having its own alibi for being here
each eavesdropping on the one behind   the derelict
one   the faded one that the brome is already erasing
with a slight push toward all the small predators
and martyrs in the thicket   all the six-legged lives
we'll never know or understand   their minds like
sonograms of a consciousness beyond design
and containment   open like grass to the sky.

BIODIVERSITY IS THE MOTHER OF ALL BEAUTY

in memory of Judy Davis

when I think of blood drops and little hurts
entering a field   filling the field
when I think of dandelions off their leashes
and the Noh play of dragonflies   airborne
red and metallic blue   light as silk

when I think that one sigh was the progenitor
of all life   that the binding of oxygen
and hydrogen is the most erotic calligraphy
that every thought   human and otherwise
                        is an astronomical unit
that each is star-laced to its very core

when I think that inside every genome there
is a line of sight that surrounds the earth
that perception holds the evanescence
                of all things within itself
that atoms are in a perpetual state of bliss

when I think that deer move elegantly between
trees like the great tea master Rikyū
did among his bowls   that a deep-sea coral
off the Hawaiian Islands is 4000 years old

when I think of parallel universes colonizing
the edges of birdsong   when I think that
        synaesthesia is the language of God
that flesh covers a wider and deeper pilgrimage

when I sit here knowing this is a dying world
nothing could be more effortless   more sacred
than this sleepy forest at dawn.

A Feral Trance

mid-July   September walking towards us
scar by scar   mosh pit of jellyfish swaying
in moonlight near the coast   moss moving
through the city   picking up the pace now
on damp summer nights   while we slide back
and forth across our dreams like nerves
                    in a pane of glass

what happens in the other world happens here first
and always at this hour   embroidered on unwoven
cloth   frayed and turned to dust before
it's remembered   before the sun rises
                    and the dew appears

we live in the omission of ourselves   in the unwindowed
areas that have no interpretation   no bright exegesis
to welcome the mind   a feral trance of dark spaces
which we inhabit beside our bodies   the dead with us
there   praising and stickling   choiring down to muteness
                    by morning

all night our every pulse is bisected by the thin blades
of God's black antennae   trying to suss out the singularity
of our intent   while we lie in bed increasing our force
field every hour   our unconscious oscillations heard
as laments   glowing like foxfire   carried off
                    along the earth's axis

carried away like lightdrift across rooftops   lunar and
transfigured   millennial every other minute
blown eastward into the shapes of waves   circumscribed
by shorelines   all dark underneath   all ungathered
and fathomed by absence   the undertow of morning
taking us down one more time   one last look
at the backwash of our dreams   before our veins are latched
latched tight and woken.

COLLECTING ANTLERS

for Barbara

the Masters of Moonlight are almost classical   almost wise
            chording veins and nerves across the forest floor
a little night music from the ground cover   a few melodic
                        lines darksome and processional

the moon glistens and the landscape glistens back   moon
at the salt lick   stars like fingernails in the flesh   trees far
from the trailhead   sleeved in northern light   mosquito hawks
in the low places   some in the high   with their gauzy hearts
and resinous blood   following their own zodiac into the brush
mating under the sign of Horus   *the distant one.*

                        *

sun above you all day as you walked the earth   clouds head
to tail   fortune there to fasten and silver the edges of your stride
                        gods heroes and beasts spread out
equally across the land   spirit-worn paths in all directions
intersected with poplars and the iron in your body
its magnetic theology pointing to the boreal axis

your *clothes wet with the blue air* to quote Wang Wei
moving through the seamless life of things to quote the Jack pine

you tramped about all afternoon collecting antlers   those
messages you keep for yourself   parchment white   with
incantations pinging each bone from the inside
with each one something approaches and lingers next to you
something the soul understands   warmth the soul needs
to hold onto   the verb *to be*   the un and becoming we all
experience in the end   the dead and risen life
                        its schism and ease

as you hiked along   the aperture of light gradually began to close
night regrouped quietly in the hollows   beginning to retell
its story   its eight chapters   still addressing our former lives
when we were elemental   when our minds had yet to appear
and our every movement was a yearning of carbon
a swooning of hydrogen   our hunger to be bodied in form.

*

Venetian mask of one in the morning   beaked and blackened
by Acheronian flames   the unborn proliferating in the weeds
the moon-soaked earth grazing on lines of scripture in its sleep
the lake gleaming between this far world and the next   like Polaris
           shining through 434 light years to reach your eye

the magpies have all gone home hours ago   also ants
like a Japanese poem of six hundred characters   rolled up
and hidden in the earth till morning   constellations like a pinch
of salt thrown over your shoulder   the campfire waving its red
and yellow flags and just beyond its circle of light a lynx
or a thought moving about in the shadows

the lacquer of sunlight had finally melted away   undercoating
of ancient animals showing through like painted saints on a wall
saints pulling in the quietude to surround you   to bring you slumber
the antlered dream of twelve tines   twelve zodiacal vanishing
points in your skin   each one leading to what is unspoken
to the whisper of a whisper   to the breath of grass greening
the invisible   your last and final footstep before sleep.

In the Wilderness

death of language by a billion blades of grass
a billion cuts along every word   yet no reason
for regret   no reason to address the situation

night like mist coming off black jade   stars on their
red ride along the vein   wolves prowling the woods
with sunlight bright on the pads of their feet
white birches over all creation.

Kraken Mare

I died among unfurling ferns and calyxes
my white throat laid bare during dark hours
blood drained   my voice crimped and pinched away

at the end I could hear blackbirds in their eggs
                                    slow rub of flesh against shell
I could hear mice open their gaze   see an iambic
light crossing the ground   having exited my body

all night a hobbled rain had fallen upon insect
erotica in the hedges   I could see their archetypal
hooks and genitalia attached with microfilaments
a sexuality riven by a breath given and a breath taken

I could sense an angel standing beside me
its thoughts elsewhere   looking into the distance
thinking about the dim wash of tide against
the shoreline of Kraken Mare   a lake
of hydrocarbons on Titan   its every nerve
unoccupied   its mind of motherese
black-winged   mumping that silence.

2010

it was a different place   a different time
when life was just another superstition
a stuttering of clouds above a hurting world
when every moment was like every wave
flesh-capped   inconsolable
unquenchable   waning to deeper thirst

there was the immense weight of naïveté
bearing down on water   the pluvial lapse
of thought falling into lakes and rivers
streams overflowing with inexperience
                              surface tensions
of what was already forgotten

there was the unendurable never-end
of breezes casting sunlight across the eye
blue skies   one after another   settling
into the body   a lap robe of fire
for every sexual intent   each of us
separated from the other by a thin scrim
of primaveral longing   green shoots
of a widening distance between thought
                              and deed

there were still gods in those days
celestial privations furred tight to the bone
panicles of neurons imagining Kàbbalahs
sweet sweet arcana leaning into the mind
into the mind's dependency on a scrap of flesh
a tincture of blood

back then every day was a changeling
and dying was simple   it felt like having someone
else's dog miss you   a dog you've never met
although the pain was sometimes staggering
you felt better in the end   like the trace of a lost
gesture behind motion itself   your voice unbuttoning
slowly   light-sprung above the trees.

LINES WRITTEN BENEATH A STONE

like the Emperor Lo-Yang seeing a supernova
I watch the starved aster open its white flower
and know there's no going back to men.

BITE DOWN LITTLE WHISPER

1.

the sky cradles an absent blood   silence of washed
veins through the trees   bloodlines flushed out
                               and carried away

hematic glyphs written once in the air and erased

we are stained by the invisible in the lowering day
by the arterial blush of the world   meanwhile
the ghosts of our fallen hair rise up to heaven
our shed skin follows us through room after room

meanwhile our thin eyelids open and close
our home disappears   and reappears
as the sum of our vacant ontology

pale ache beneath our tongues   pale metaphysics

The land that is nowhere, that is our true home
I use these words as talismans
shining syllables to hang in the branches
for luck   for chimes when the wind returns.

2.

late hours among the weeds   grass top-heavy
with exoskeletons   film noir and animal weights

cats beginning to head out across fields
dusk banked up against their fur like dark birds

a maggot with a gondola's long shine over water
skimming the surface of a mouse lying in the brome

a doe standing still in the acquittal of light
each leg holding a presolar energy
                    and a mouthful of air

and we're there most days as witnesses
pressing our headaches against windowpanes
watching and waiting for time to gather us in
waiting for strange brushstrokes across our hearts
our hands just out of reach   our sight laid low
                                    in the guise

death filling in the blanks as holy writ and a steady grace
nothing profane   micro-organisms written
as sacred text on the painted tissue of things as they curl
as they die and are assimilated   curl and fall.

3.

the end of day is a tapestry of one thread
laid flat across the landscape   a thin string
pulling sparrows up and over black hills

evening comes   dharma of bruised lips
blowing out the candles   loosening light
and time around the heart

so that night is a brief hurt among the illuminations
and sleep is an anatomy lesson without a body.

4.

midnight or thereabouts   clouds gathering
like pressed flowers in a weightless book

a few stars on black paper   a few missing

among pine trees I've built a small life
a temporary narrative   ogham cuts in solitude
my fire swaying   deepening nature's blush
night's drift carrying that shine away

a night with a bad tooth in its jaw
the ache snug between ferns
a whisper of pain   telegenic among
hawk's beard and groundsel
among intercessions of the vetchling

there is no metaphor for such inflictions
so bite down little whisper   black incisor
right there where the inaccessible meets stillness
where yesterday's words draw the light in

bite down and sit tight   just there
where my fingers look for solitude
in the landscape   along mossy
stitches in the wood   along jinx
and orifice   dung and honey
where our shudders first ruptured
                              into language
language into deeper sleep.

5.

camo of deep woods   black and grey
double dyed on quietude   tincted
with shadows of coyotes blading by
eviscerators flat against the breeze

hunter and hunted bloodied   processional
Vedic lip-synch of teeth on flesh
If the slayer thinks that he slays, and the slain
thinks that he is slain, neither knows the
ways of truth

so bite down little whisper   right there
where we live layered between form
                              and formlessness

where words from the Upanishads
are like bedclothes laid on the living
and the dead ... *neither knows*
the ways of truth   I kneel to this
every time   without knowing why

on nights like this it gives me comfort

on nights when I would rather
be a rabbit orbiting a celestial hunger
lost in the clover's gravitational pull
or one of those crows high in the branches
above me   just out of God's reach
splinters of sleep passing through their bodies
each feather trembling in its separate dream
each shiver holding twelve skies.

6.

I tend my fire   a little lip at flame's end
a little curl of speech turned to smoke and ash
something redemptive in the burning wood
almost spoken of in the moment   almost heard

moon rising   white cathedral where we all
eventually go to pray   our only church
when we try to hush the dog and hush the rose
listening for improvisations of the one silence
one emptiness   ear to stone

I tend my fire   a little galaxy at flame's end
a little curl of sidereal time turned to smoke and ash
burning dry sticks and branches   a reclusive
iconography   melancholia and its sacrament
                              drear and aura

drowse of the absolute somewhere above me
cloistered and nodding off among microbes
among changelings and starvelings
incessantly drifting   little fadeaways
on their deep journeys through the virga

seated beneath the overhang of pine boughs
my grief and ignorance want for nothing
feed off an absence   autolytic and bittersweet
feed off a synaptic loss   that space between
two words   where our souls will finally
              be tonsured and nail-clipped
our hearts sewn shut over our eyes

tonight I bow my head   tonight the darkness
bows back at me from its shining abyss

meanwhile a chrysalis retools its enzymes

meanwhile grasses grow along the deer path
each a copy of a beautiful mother.

ABSENCES IN GRASS ROOMS

night like a bladebox   day like a begging bowl
roses and traffic in their proper places
ants numbering along   one of Audubon's songs
in the hedges   roots of fleabane tightening
around the right ventricle of every shadow

for the moment I live quietly in unfinished rooms of grass
off Highway 236   where the water goes when it's tired
where each stone whispers in its own ear
as the backcloth of sky sweeps hallowed ground
as maggots perform their autopsies
with a fierce and methodical grace

quietude is my livelihood   my stub and coin
now at hand   now that mornings are long
only the mummery of ravens to be heard
only that and the breathing of nonbeing
against the bark of every tree.

late sunlight   a cubit of cloud above
                              the poplars
an arm's length of rain drifting off
and a contrail heading east to the Atlantic
blue water waiting there with its one joy
and its ten billion lamentations

like a craze of fingerlings eventually we'll
pass through the gabled end of the self
and fall into elsewhere   into the real
world of things and disappear

but not now   now the anons drop-stitch
each step through the undergrowth
their six legs and mouthparts carefully
practicing a sublime aesthetic

but not now   now there's a brush of deer
painting slow movements in the spruce grove
now there are three dragonflies doing turnarounds
in the air   fibre optics of their eyes following
the altarlight of their prey into absolution.

the bees have been written and read
returned to their hives   I sit still
without a god at the cardinal points
without an angel wearing a beard of gold in its hair

I sit with a shave of light low in the west
with stars pinched shut   origamic moon folded in half
tail lights of fireflies   this hour
like the slatch between two heartbeats

taxonomy of an irreplaceable love drifting by
as a riparian text   all mist and sex
                       all pillows and blood
while far off a dog barks at some maleficium
some small evil grinding its leather teeth
clockwise then counter-clockwise in the dark

I sit with absences in grass rooms
while field mice perform their black ops in weedlight
while a heron bends down to lace up the water
tightly around each ankle
while the river carries its slow freight of genes
even in meaninglessness   even in that immortality.

The Alchemical Lion Is Green and Devours the Sun

Dewdrops,
let me cleanse
in your brief,
sweet waters
these dark hands of life.

~ Bashō

your long wait is over   finally there's a bit
of dust on the road   a blackbird in the sky
pupae scarved in Fibonacci numbers
spirals of DNA growing out of emptiness
a new crop of bacterial life in the ditchwater

at long last you've cottoned onto the backstory
of Bashō's obsession with dew and rain
with the antiquity of rain falling
                  among pine trees
why Sōgi wrote *I place my trust in the dew.*

                  *

bright morning   the sun scything back
the dew from hundreds of stones in the field
each shut tight like a glovebox
each containing a mirror with just the trace
of a breath across its surface   a newborn's
breath   to be picked up at birth and carried
across the earth   outliving any meaning

your headache arrives the way an earpiece
brings you music through a thin black wire
a countertheme to your morning's peace
with a pain indistinguishable from allegory
identical to that unnamed story
which never appeared in the Aesopica
which was never printed   never passed
                  on by any oral tradition.

*

if you were a god you would be generous
to a fault   providing a blood
meal for every mite   a statue of Tiberius
for every hive   a Bernini collarbone
for every bride   a baroque song
to accompany each shearwater falling to earth

your mind would constantly scull around your body
passing through its own slow mystery   edges
rain-worn and ragged from absolution
you would think if cornered ˙ knowing each thought
leaves a scar   a tear in fleshtime

if you were a god each breath would be
                                    an incremental sigh
your vocal cords syncopated   archetyped   retrofitted
and veined through every word ever spoken
in your chest would be a crayon heart
perpetually beating outside the lines
you would be the god you always wanted
and at length find serenity   shoulders squared

sitting and then lying on the riffling grass.

*

softly softly the dew sings to the root
root sings to the bee   the bee sings applying
propolis to the sun and so the day is made
cloud-scented and glistening forth
with an undertone of pale blue
like the symbiotic tint of opposable thoughts

today your footsteps finger the rosary
of your spine   little prayer   little prayer
each with a Faustian regard for knowledge
trying to understand the momentary nexus
of aesthetics and death   how the centuries
turn on a branch and fall   turn once and fall

it's taken you the better part of a lifetime
to accept the spirit of things broken
to come to terms with the hemorrhaging
of each genome   to the grinding of roses
on bone   to learn that life is marginal
                                        to existence
to watch the green lion devour the sun.

                    *

in the understory   in that space below
the canopy of branches and leaves   just where
light fades   where light begins   in that high altar
light there's always a moment in suspension
a moment that has always been there
                        unused and immaculate

you've noticed it before   away from the noise
of the world   away from the atmospherics
                                        of Paradise
no sins or blessings there   no Elysium sheen
on a god's brow   no soul to fuss with

anima dannata   anima beata

just an invisibility colourless as dew   an outtake
from the Hadean   a vacancy frescoed
on emptiness   nothing to puzzle out
                    to unwind   to unbend

just being itself   beingness without visitation
without revelation or redemption
and over time you'll learn to whisper
to that distance   to that lack of distance
affix it to your soul when your back is turned

to place your trust in the dew.

THE LIGHT OF UNOCCUPIED MEMORY

Radiance and Counterpoint

for Wayne Boucher

a louche moon on a still night
carrion beetles in pre-op
no great anxieties among the dead

no frenzy in the ecotone tonight
only this business of walking here
surrounded by the casual dress code
of the horseweed   by antediluvian
laments distilled   refined
circling as gnats and invisibilities
lovers that bite and fly away

it's a long drop between one footstep
and another   a long fall between one
                    thought and the next
what separates each is the dark decide
of things absent   like the dying rabbit
far off in the distance lying in hackles
of grass   or a bit of sparrowsdown
caught on a twig a continent away
that interconnectiveness oiling
our joints   anointing our limbs
allowing for every measure of movement.

                    *

only the masters were wise enough
to bow to moths drifting about
                    like prayer papers
or to foxes dubbing blood to motion

only they painted the blue of things
that lean hard against our infirmities
only they used the shy tempera of birdsong
and the red opiates found among
the clot-brown roots of the locust trees

they were the ones like lacewings
that floated on   full of grace
as they dovetailed with the landscape
aspired to what was lowly   black water
at the roots of things   black syllables
of a skeined prophesy wrapped ninefold
and ninefold again around their hearts
like pyrographic silk   each word burnt
in with the smallest flame   the largest
hope to lose any semblance of wisdom.

*

life has an apparitional hue   pale and ethereal
like a stripe of moonlight on a deer's back
to this we pray   conceding to loss
preening our awayness between our words

our entire lives are lived in the Dutch interior
of a nodding prayer   as gold specks
of devastation fall and collect on our skin
as our frayed bodies are finally jerry-rigged
to silence and set adrift

silence arrives tonight without a deity   with only
the supplication of itself on offer to these hours
Soon silence will have passed into legend
as Jean Arp said   the dismantling of silence
one absence at a time   one wandering interval
                              of a sorrowful realm

silence is a conjunction of premonitions
bodings and unendings of perception   a witching
that summons us from our distractions
our amusements   from the sweet old human
world which fails us each day.

this planet is made of Etruscan clay
mountain and plain   rock and tile
a thin bloodline opened around its centre
from which we emerged in parentheses

subtextual and luminous with secrets
with mysteries   pre-reflective sacraments
wordlessly given   wordlessly taken

we arrived with our heartbeats
anchored firmly to the earth   scree-held
our flesh over-rehearsed   bone and sinew
radiance and counterpoint
overlapping in endless gestures
our organs soft-spoken   shape-shifting
                    throughout the Tertiary
our minds neither here nor there
our sixth sense working like a spider
in the undergrowth   scissoring light

tonight I tread that ancient bloodline
with time's ashes kiting overhead
with mice at the end of their valedictions
the snap of a chrysalis in the bushes

coyote synergy in the hills   air-coloured eyes
Talmudic curl of their tongues behind each
                        and every bark
coyotes   coydogs   their phantom limbs
carrying them back to the Pleistocene each night
back to their petroglyphs   nails on stone.

ETERNITY

landscape leached of description
all words moved to one side
            radiant babies in the hills

nothing for them to do now but enter the mist
two breaths   three   then circle high above
the earth   waiting for mothers to be born.

Writing on Black Silk

clouds in lowercase   moths on their
maiden flights   and grief ever returning
from somewhere high up in the poplar trees

it's 2004 and I'm on the Yangtze River
where Li Po fell from his boat and drowned
trying to embrace the reflection of the moon
                              in the flowing water

same moon tonight   same reflection
shadows of our masters still metastasizing
somewhere in the places of power
improvisations of mist still ineffable
stars still creating myth out of shrugs of light
indifferent to our attempts at divination
indifferent to our applied mathematics

tonight I'm a bit of pigment in a T'ang scroll
rusted blemish that bleeds through
                              from the future
bamboo along the shore brushed
dark and darker   the mountains
raising their effigies and fetishes to heaven

ten million bales of black silk have unfurled
between the gorges   the Celestials
like paper fish glow and float to the surface
their words for our sorrows unknown
to us still   their secrecy on every subject
                              intricate and unwavering

a river crocodile slides under our boat
ink lines of its lips fixed in a permanent smile
its clinched armour a counterpane
for an arterial sleep   blood's dodge
in unlit waters   someone's heart at ease.

tonight the earth has all the metabolism of a single
candle left burning on a sill   I'm standing
in that hesitation before all prayer   where
pheromones are released from the sexual pairing
of thought and moonlight

I wait for you here   while a coyote's footsteps
circle me like paper ships on water   while grass
is drenched with falling voices that once collected
                                        at the heliopause
and owls shine the nacre behind their wide eyes

I wait patiently for you among all the transgressive
fictions the forest has to offer   under a quench
of clouds and a soft breeze blowing through
the exoskeleton of the Buddha   lying empty
and mindful in the weeds

I wait while night nervously bites the inside
of its cheek every time headlights appear
                                        at the horizon
every time the ambient air burns brightly

even the neuronic flash of thought is too radiant
that winnowing   that crossing into language

there are elephants whispering at my feet
from the other side of the earth

there are lions that say goodbye very slowly.

All Souls' Night

wind like the turning pages of a grimoire
with no pleasantries in the margins
no illumination
between the words   no interference
                    from sight or thought

only Lascaux light at the roots of things
to guide us along
only our pulse lapping against distance
our souls always seeking the horizon
its grandeur and after-effect
that moment lived
at the very front of beyond

our souls are one nanometre thick
lamplit and tucked in
a mere musk beneath our dermis
flushing at any elegiac sound
any essence dilated   bellied out
passing through our bodies

overhead there are clouds sliding along
like blood on waxed paper   flowing back
to that prayer in the Late Bronze Age
the one about drought and rain
about the mind's camera obscura
that pinpoint of light projecting
gods onto the cave wall of the retina

it comes with our animal soul
that unapologetic ache in our words
generations of petitions answered
and unanswered
wild heaven and its aftermath.

Beneath a Feline Moon

the night sky is over us   under-wrapped in sedge
down the street someone is turning a deadbolt
                              turning the world on its axis
in the nearby woods a cat can see the moon channelled
into the landscape and clouds like low hanging fruit
swaying to the music of loosestrife

no one is about at this hour except the ginger cat and I
the world feeling our footsteps as strokes of thought
                    half a centimetre above the soil

yet neither of us is thinking   neither of us have
mass or weight   no mentation to blemish
the moonlight   no destinations to our journeys
                              upon the earth.

Little House of Misfortune

in the sanctuary of book and reader   clouds slake in Terran light
filigree and fade   in this refuge where the mist has fallen   its blood
lying unbuttoned on the ground   where the grass is written in Linear A
and elk come right up to the words and pause   unafraid

in this place where every sentence is a cradlesong   I've learnt to speak
softly in elisions   in omissions   to walk in approximations
sleep in scalages   finding the weight and dimensions of language
                    in its translation of flesh

in the shelter of pages opened   I've listened to the far-off sound
of endless photographs of the ocean slapping against the shore
I've watched the limnings of sparrows ascending like John Dee's
Enochian alphabet   their angel wings   their paper striae tensing
around incantations of flight

in the impermanence of paper I've underlined the faint respiration
of wolves writing on their own breath   dog-eared the coalescing
of lexicon and taxon   highlighted the offload of species into lyricism
the breaking and entering of their petitions into our consciousness

in the opiates of books I've taken leave of my senses and found them
again   sanctified   I've discovered the stemma of convergences curled
up in margins   felt bindings straining to hear my fingers turn the page
found bookmarks separating dream from soil   and in all this I've come
to understand the visitational pain of punctuation
                    how it bruises and injures syntactic skin

I've learnt that the period at the end of each sentence is called the Little
House of Misfortune   its black jawline of frame and door slamming shut
over and over   that beadsmen live there   praying for all the words
that have gone astray   all the texts that have been bodied by neglect
erased or deleted   finally syllabled by a darkness that's nonlexical
and motherless   brought to naught   lost in Munch light.

Fair and Square of the Flesh

in the breath of aging flesh   in the flesh
where sunlight is the shadow's shadow
where the arcana of bright fires darken
and pupate beneath our skin

in the realpolitik of our diminishing flesh
hived sunlight warms the monograms
of timelines and veins   follows
the stretch marks of heartbeats   little veldts
of muscle living on the heat   diseases supping
on the burn   translating their Latin names
                                in our blood

in the smile of the flesh   in the expressions
of the flesh all our conjurations
all our whistlings in the dark mean nothing
all of Milton's warring angels cannot
protect us   the good ones nor the bad

in the beauty of the flesh   in the enchantment
of the flesh   with glamour's apostles
salamandered between the kindle and flames
of our laments   with death growing there
till it acquires the weight of a single carat
till it gathers the energy it takes to look at a rose

in the fair and square of the flesh   in the cabal
of the flesh I lay my head down each night
a low-rider through sleep   almost touching
the earth as I go   homesick for my waking body
its signal fires sanctified and burning low
like sunlight dropping beneath the horizon
and one person there watching that scar fade
that cut of light burn free of the flesh.

Marginalia

it was about something else
something in the clade of events
a jotting down in the margins
of flesh   perhaps it was something
about dying
about the midsection of each death folded
once around a drop of rain and allowed
to fall back to earth

perhaps it was about this rainy afternoon
slipshod and pressed down by atmospheres
stacked one atop the other   like wax skies
made by Madame Tussaud   half melted
from the warm physiques of birds

perhaps its concerns were simply about
this moment itself
antennae in the grass
a wisp of snipe in the air
continents adrift   nothing contextual
womb-moulded bodies everywhere

I imagine each note like a cylinder seal
rolled into our tissues
to become part of a dark marginalia
the anatomy holds for a time   read
and translated each night
by some personification of fate

every message a laceration salted by Fortuna's
breath   blood drawn up through each letter
each word burnt away by sight.

THE LIGHT OF UNOCCUPIED MEMORY

1.

I head west by seven feet   north by one   standing where I stood
a moment ago   listening to the creek's daily grind of thought
on stone   watching a crow's scarification of the sky
early morning   blood baptizing blood in hollows
and on mountaintops   clouds building their vast landscape
tearing it down every few minutes   rebuilding it again

hard not to tug on the heart's sleeve and move on   looking
for solace in motion's narrative   in those fast and easy phrases
that define   difficult staying centered in the almost reality
of this moment   in the almost world spinning on God's dime

all the apologues say to tread carefully   that every footstep
is a reason to remain still   that all movement is dangerous
yet we get on with our lives   having no choice
everything explained and unexplained   the future already
a memory   collecting in the folds of things.

2.

these paper birches are half remembered by yesterday's rain
half understood by sunlight   I feel at home among them
peering through their windows caked with dust   looking down
into the soil's registry   where all our names are written
the secret ones we've waited all of our lives to hear

for hours I've been listening for a unit of language   a syllable
or sign   any diaphanous nod towards meaning
but the forest has no words   whatever it had to say was said
in the late Miocene   the rest has been white syntax   the way
the wind speaks   a mouthful of leaves and a luminous stutter

the treetops sway holding onto hawk's breath   a lynx pads by
digesting a rabbit's whispers   beetles and spiders work
the grass   here's hoping they find their way safely home
to that reliquary light deep in the foliage   light without
impurities   without height or width   without place
                    the light of unoccupied memory.

3.

each day swallows its wafer   drinks its wine   receiving
blessings from somewhere out of the canopy's green chasuble
meanwhile wounds are in the details and asters are gifting
meanwhile history bends the sedge just a little as it passes

an afternoon soft to the touch   like second-hand gossamer
a drop cloth that holds the visible and invisible
slightly worn along the creases   where life meets fate
where the lower powers tick on between the weeds

an afternoon like swansdown adrift on water   time scattered
by hand between rocks and trees   a hand as large   as thin
as a fly's wing   little hand make me an hour in which to shine
make me a minute in which I can see   a moment in which the
exquisite tightens its grip on my all too human heart
and the weight of the beast becomes the weight of the mind.

4.

I'd love to have the wolf's edgeless sense of self   to understand
the weather's assignations in the underbrush   to see through a raven's
eye spread out like air between the branches   to be moss breathing in
the green blush of consciousness from the forest floor   to know how
it feels to be this monarch fluttering by   this *painted child of dirt*

on the other hand being human is underwork   drop stitch and intersect
transcendence and pinprick   the mind's shadow is always the shadow
of something else   never of itself   there's the ache and the heartache
little curses   small banes in the blood flow   familiar things

like a pond the mind plants its reeds   washes its stones and waits
only we haven't any idea what it's waiting for   not a clue
even a parable can't help us   even the land   even the wind
can't rouse an answer   wind through the evergreens
                like unleavened souls through *Purgatorio*.

5.

quietus of a clear-cut   numberless ants running about the
fatwood with black cutlery in their mouths   ferns grab
onto the shade and hold tight   while saplings turn their thoughts
into leaves and the soil offers up its one belief   its one and only
which keeps the earth spinning in endless space

sun overhead with nothing to say   its wisdom on the q.t.
in the form of a single golden breath falling on amness and its
countless minutia   each ray an air-kiss and a pat on the back
I sit among birch shadows without that affection   waiting for
an invitation   a call in from the other side of a grass blade

my mind feels like a dry riverbed filled with ghost water   it flows
with the light of unoccupied memory   nothing to think   nothing
to know   only silences sliding between the silences   only ghost
fish   restfully swimming downstream   away from the future.

Unborn

Charon folding water   Morpheus folding dreams
a dark road ahead of us   a dark forest with whispers
where the leaves should be   not clouds overhead
but an afterlife   not wind but a laying on of hands

evening came down from the mountain to reassure us
with its presence   its footprints without footsteps
sight without eyes   it held us and we felt like grass
moving through grass   like a sigh along a riverbed

we stood in each other's shadow   lay in each other's arms
vertebrates   invertebrates   every possible form
and like numina we drew sleep from stones   breath from fire
like virga we sang of a reality deeper than the mind.

WINTERING

the heartweight of snow falling
among dead pine trees
a crow's yardwork abandoned
Judgement Day come and gone

Acherontic wind from the outlands
wolves moving through the forest
like sewn dust
          interlaced and unfaltering

two and a half days of whiteout
February unworkable   leeching
every apophatic reason
      from God's solitary
appointments in the hills

three wishes calcifying
on every branch   our hopes
like wiped blades inserted
someplace in the landscape
where we never go

our penitential Book of Secrets
unlatching its covers momentarily
releasing a few illegible words
to the albescent text of the storm

a few thin syllables   glossolalia
the work of wings against glass
little scratches   indistinct   falling
like flakes of snow
like the pain of auspicious things.

Shudder and Climb

1.

early hours   moon hidden in the wings   the dead in their small
apartments   bent heavily over paperwork till dawn   little night things
set adrift   feral cries   sleep-driven just beyond sleep

I'm waiting for the preordained visitant to appear   the aphasic breath
that licks the soul clean   shadow's understudy   eternity's beautiful dog
that comes to wash the humanity from our blood
                                        just for a moment or two

in the hope that we can see the further reaches of our being
the going to and coming back   enriched by our journey   by journey's
end among arteries of lost voices in the flesh.

2.

whatever has been thought or felt was first written down
before the Holocene   beneath pigment applied to a rock face
yellow ochre in the shape of a horse
or an ibex   still we putter about thinking ourselves new
only human of course   only animal   our phrasal teeth gnawing
on windfallen bones from someone else's
idiom   still we're happy enough on the good days
                                        bleeding out on the bad

burnishing our words   we hold them up   expecting miracles
                    radiance at the darkest moment of the night
without realizing each night enters holy orders long before sunrise
martyrdom and fade-out   a cowl's melancholia
pulled down quietly over the hours   all the sin-eaters in synch
before day breaks   before we begin our sequence of supplications
little prayers for the long commute
to a near-truth   for all the goodbyes between names and destinations.

3.

our sense of loss is visceral   a fine tuning of dross in the body
a sharp sting felt on the other side of perception
like silhouettes calving in the taiga
                              just beyond our consciousness

all those shadows that will one day be stitched into our skin
refolded   slid into our veins

all the while longing for our wounds to be removed   pocketed in red
linen and carried away   to be stealthily hidden
                              behind a cat's hair or a grain of sand

longing for an incorruptible redemption to carry us forth
in a raven's beak   in a rabbit's foot
bearing us through evergreens in a slow waltz and glide
to that place between our eyes   where the soul first muddled
into a physical world   first experienced thought
its apparitional flow and pulse   its low burn into our tissues
its fire and stake   its postpartum auto-da-fé.

4.

there are deer asleep in the hills   their slow breathing
                        lifting up the tell of a thing lost
something with lamentations on its back
something made of belief and unbelief in equal measure

there are also angels sending messages from stone to stone
with mezzo heartbeats but no chain of command   no controller
                        no Lord of Illuminations and Afflictions

we exist between deer and angels   between earth and earth's
reflection   we originate out of the soughing and reshuffling
of wind and cloud   cloud and blood

tonight the clouds circumnavigate a sprig of bitterweed
broken   lying on the ground   all of its rooms darkened now
all its doors unlatched   we stand on its roof to watch
the stars   enthralled   mum   caught up in eternity

and they look back at us   like God we want to say   but don't.

5.

under the child-rearing stars   beneath the welkin petalled with black flames
there are times when the self is inconceivable
when whatever was made of mind and body is unmade   laid to rest
a bit of grey ash on a scry's prophetic thermal

here deep in the forest   in the stillness of ecocide
in the quietude between spruce trees   when absence redeems you
when the world is rising and leaving
                                        when you've forgotten your name
forgotten the wistful knot of air that is your spirit
that's when the ancients say you'll reach the bottom of things
and start upwards again   on the bodings of an ascent
beyond the grief of your infirmities   that's good medicine
the ache of return outside the self
the winged offspring of your cells pressing flight
a dark drop of genesis for the soul's shudder and climb.

ACKNOWLEDGEMENTS

I would like to thank the Canada Council for their continuing support.

Thanks to the editors of the following magazines and anthologies where some of these poems appeared: *70 Canadian Poets* (Oxford University Press), *Arc, Arts East, Cerise Press* (France/United States), *Contemporary International Poetry: Canadian Poetry Special Edition* (China), *Eighteen Bridges, Grain, Ice Floe* (United States), *Prairie Fire, The Best Canadian Poetry in English 2009* and *The Best Canadian Poetry in English 2010* (Tightrope Books), The Canadian Parliamentary Poet Laureate's Website, *The Literary Review of Canada, The Malahat Review.*

Thanks also to Glen Downie (Tall Tree Press) for publishing "Apocrypha" as a broadside. And as always a deep thanks to Barry Dempster for his eyes and heart.

NOTES

URSA IMMACULATE:
Julii. One of the oldest families of Ancient Rome. Julius Caesar and Gaius Julius Caesar Augustus were members of this family.

MADONNA OF THE DIAPHANOUS LIFE:
Thrace. Home of the Thracians, an ancient Indo-European people that lived in Southeastern Europe. A group of ascetics called the Ctistae lived there, where they served as prophets and priests.
Skellig. The Great Skellig, a steep rocky island off the coast of County Kerry, Ireland. From the seventh century the island was a centre of monastic life for Irish Christian monks for about six hundred years.

FORESIGHT BY EARTH:
Nibiru. Also called Planet X, a planet or planetoid that will supposedly have a collision with the Earth at some future date.
Olduvai Gorge. A deep ravine in the Great Rift Valley of east Africa. It's one of the most important paleoanthropological sites in the world and has been extremely important in our understanding of early human evolution.
geomancy. From the ancient Greek meaning "foresight by earth." It's a method of divination that interprets markings on the ground or the patterns formed by tossed handfuls of sand, soil, or rocks.

MAGNUM MYSTERIUM:
piquerism. The sexual practice of perforating the skin of another person.

APPARITIONAL HOUND:
Khandava. The Khandava Forest, an ancient forest mentioned in the Hindu epic *Mahabharata*.

THE GARDEN IS SECRETIVE ... :
Abydos. One of the most sacred and ancient cities of Egypt.

FOR THE PURE MOTHER BEE:
latrias. Prayers directed only to the Holy Trinity. An internal form of worship, rather than outward ceremonies.

FIRST FOLIO OF THE UNWRITTEN:
abacination. To blind someone by holding a red-hot metal plate before the eyes.

BITE DOWN LITTLE WHISPER:
The land that is nowhere, that is our true home. From Chang Po-tuan, Chinese alchemist of the eleventh century.

LITTLE HOUSE OF MISFORTUNE:
Enochian alphabet. An alphabet that appeared in the sixteenth century. Dr John Dee and Sir Edward Kelly claimed that the alphabet was transmitted to them by angels.

THE LIGHT OF UNOCCUPIED MEMORY:
painted child of dirt. From *Epistle to Dr Arbuthnot* by Alexander Pope: "Who breaks a butterfly upon a wheel?
Yet let me flap this bug with gilded wings,
This painted child of dirt that stinks and stings ... "

Don Domanski was born and raised on Cape Breton Island and now lives in Halifax, Nova Scotia. He is the author of eight books of poetry and the winner of the 2007 Governor General's Award, the Atlantic Poetry Prize and the 2008 Lieutenant Governor of Nova Scotia Masterworks Arts Award. Published and reviewed internationally, his work has been translated into Czech, French, Portuguese, Arabic, Chinese and Spanish.